MARSHMALLOW COOKBOOK
FOR BEGINNERS

100 CREATIVE AND SWEET MARSHMALLOW RECIPES

Grace White

TABLE OF CONTENTS

INTRODUCTION

There are so many ways to use marshmallows for your favorite breakfast, main course, holiday treat, or dessert. Whether you choose a bag of mini marshmallows, big marshmallows, or a jar of marshmallow fluff, this book has all the best marshmallow recipes that are gooey, sticky, and oh-so-sweet. The best part about these sticky-good recipes is that many of them qualify as no-bake, and some only require a handful of ingredients!

BREAKFAST AND BRUNCH

1. Cocoa infused with marshmallow

Makes: 1

INGREDIENTS:
- 1 cup of milk.
- 1 cinnamon stick.
- ¼ teaspoon nutmeg.
- 1 tablespoon unsweetened cocoa powder.
- 1-ounce chocolate chips.
- 1 dropper of coconut oil.
- Mini marshmallows.
- 1 shot of Cinnamon whiskey

INSTRUCTIONS:
a) In a medium-sized saucepan, heat the milk.
b) Simmer over low heat with the cinnamon and nutmeg for 10 minutes.
c) Stir in cocoa powder.
d) Let it simmer for a few minutes before turning off the heat.
e) Combine chocolate, whiskey, coconut oil, and marshmallow in one mug.

2. **Tiramisu Shake**

Makes: 2

INGREDIENTS:
- 5 ounces Tincture
- 4 large scoops of vanilla ice cream
- ½ cup mocha
- whipped cream
- chocolate syrup
- Cocoa powder for sprinkling
- A handful of toasted marshmallows

INSTRUCTIONS:
a) Combine the tincture, ice cream, and mocha in a mixing bowl until smooth.
b) Pour into a tall glass, fill up with whipped cream, chocolate syrup, and cocoa powder, and dust with cocoa powder.
c) Garnish with marshmallows.

3. <u>Waffled S'mores</u>

Makes: 4

INGREDIENTS:
- Nonstick cooking spray
- ½ cup white whole wheat flour
- ½ cup all-purpose flour
- ¼ cup firmly packed dark brown sugar
- ½ teaspoon baking soda
- ¼ teaspoon salt
- Pinch of ground cinnamon
- 4 tablespoons unsalted butter, melted
- 2 tablespoons milk
- ¼ cup honey
- 1 tablespoon pure vanilla extract
- ¾ cup semisweet chocolate chips
- ¾ cup mini marshmallows

INSTRUCTIONS:
a) Preheat the waffle iron to medium. Coat both sides of the waffle iron grid with nonstick spray.
b) In a mixing bowl, combine the flour, brown sugar, baking soda, salt, and cinnamon. In a separate bowl, whisk together the melted butter, milk, honey, and vanilla.
c) Add the wet **INGREDIENTS:** to the flour mixture and stir until a dough forms.
d) Let the mixture stand for 5 minutes. It will be much thicker than ordinary waffle batter, but not as thick as bread dough.
e) Measure out about ¼ cup of batter and place it on one section of the waffle iron. Repeat with another ¼ cup of batter, to give you a top and a bottom for your sandwich.
f) Close the lid and cook until the waffled graham crackers are still slightly soft but cooked for 3 minutes.
g) Carefully remove the waffled graham crackers from the waffle iron. They will be quite soft, so use care to keep them intact. Allow them to cool slightly. Repeat Steps 5 to 7 with the rest of the batter.

4. Marshmallow Pancakes

Makes: 4

INGREDIENTS:
- 1 cup / 8 oz mini marshmallows
- 2 cups / 16 oz self-rising flour
- 2 cups / 16 oz milk
- 2 eggs fresh and free range
- ¼ teaspoon salt

TOPPINGS
- 2 tablespoon mini marshmallows
- maple syrup
- butter

INSTRUCTIONS:

a) Batter: add the flour, milk, eggs, and salt to a mixing bowl. Use a wooden spoon to stir till consistently combined.

b) Marshmallows: add the mini marshmallows to the pancake batter, and stir to combine.

c) Cook: spray a crepe pan with canola oil. Place on the stove and turn it to medium heat. Use a ⅓ measuring cup to spoon and pour the mixture onto the pan. Pour it straight down and keep your hand in one spot.

d) Flip: the pancakes will take 2 to 3 mins to cook on the 1st side. Watch for the bubbles that will form on the surface starting at the edges. When they work their way into the center, it is time to flip the pancakes. Slide a silicon turner under the cooked side, ensure the pancake is on the flipper, then raise your hand slightly and flip to the other side. Let this side cook for 1 to 2 mins.

e) Stack: once the pancakes are cooked, start to stack them on a serving plate. Add some mini marshmallows to the stack as you work your way up. Once at the top, spread some butter on top, sprinkle some more marshmallows on top and then drizzle the stack with maple syrup.

f) Serve: place the pancake stack on the breakfast table as a centerpiece. Or provide plates and forks for serving and let people decorate their own.

5. <u>Marshmallow Breakfast Cereal Bars</u>

Makes: 9 bars

INGREDIENTS:
- 6 tablespoons of butter
- 16 ounces bag of marshmallows
- 6 cups of cereal, mixing up the measurement through whatever cereals you choose

INSTRUCTIONS:
a) Line a 9" square baking dish with parchment paper and set aside
b) In a large microwave-safe bowl, add the butter. Heat the butter in the microwave until it melts, about 1 ½ minutes melt the butter
c) Add the marshmallow to the bowl and stir them with the melted butter. Place the bowl back into the microwave and heat for another 1 ½ minutes, watching to make sure the marshmallows don't overflow. Remove and stir. If the marshmallows aren't completely melted, you can reheat them for additional time. mixing marshmallows into melted butter
d) Now add the cereal! Mix all your favorite cereal into the marshmallow and carefully stir. You don't want to crush up all the cereal as you mix it.
e) Pour the cereal mixture into the prepared baking dish. Gently spread and press down into the pan. Try not to press too hard or they will be harder to eat. cereal bars with marshmallows
f) Allow it to set for about an hour. Cut and enjoy!

6. Chocolate & Marshmallow French Toast Roll Ups

Makes: 8 servings

INGREDIENTS:

FOR THE ROLL-UPS:
- 8 slices white sandwich bread
- ½ cup mini marshmallows
- ½ cup mini chocolate chips
- 1 Tablespoon butter

FOR THE CHOCOLATE EGG MIXTURE:
- 2 large eggs
- 3 Tablespoons milk
- ½ Tablespoon vanilla extract
- 1 Tablespoon cocoa powder

FOR THE CHOCOLATE-SUGAR MIXTURE:
- ⅓ cup granulated sugar
- 1 teaspoon cinnamon
- 1 Tablespoon cocoa powder

INSTRUCTIONS:

a) Cut the crust from each slice of bread and flatten the slice out with a rolling pin.

b) Place the mini marshmallows and the chocolate chips inside towards one end of the slice of bread.

c) Roll the bread up tightly. Repeat with the remaining slices of bread.

d) Prepare the chocolate egg mixture: in a shallow bowl, whisk together the eggs, milk, vanilla extract, and one tablespoon of cocoa powder. Stir well.

e) Prepare the chocolate-sugar mixture: on a plate, mix sugar, cinnamon, and one tablespoon of cocoa powder. Set aside.

f) Heat a skillet set over medium heat and melt the butter.

g) Dip each roll in the chocolate egg mixture, coating well, and place them into the pan. Cook them until golden brown on all sides, about 2 minutes per side. Add butter to the pan as needed.

h) Take each cooked roll from the pan and roll immediately in the chocolate-sugar mixture until completely covered in sugar.

7. Fluffernutter Oatmeal

Makes: 2 servings

INGREDIENTS:
- 1 cup quick oats
- 2 cups water
- 3-6 tablespoons creamy peanut butter, or amount to taste
- 2-4 tablespoons marshmallow fluff, or amount to taste

OPTIONAL TOPPINGS
- sliced banana or other favorite fruit
- dried fruit
- 100% pure maple syrup
- ground cinnamon
- chia seeds or other seeds or nuts

INSTRUCTIONS:
a) In a small-medium saucepan, add 2 cups water, and bring to a boil.
b) When the water is at a boil, add the 1 cup quick oats, and cook for 1 minute, stirring as it's cooking.
c) When it is done, spoon evenly into 2 bowls.
d) Add the peanut butter and marshmallow fluff and any optional toppings that you would like. Enjoy!

8. Toblerone French Toast

Makes: 2 servings

INGREDIENTS:
- 3 slices French Bread
- 2 eggs lightly beaten
- 2/3 cup milk
- 1 teaspoon vanilla extract
- 1/4 teaspoon salt
- 1 cup graham cracker crumbs
- butter
- 6 large marshmallows cut in half
- 2 full-size Toblerone bars broken into rectangles
- maple syrup for serving

INSTRUCTIONS
a) In a shallow bowl or pie plate, whisk together eggs, milk, vanilla, and salt.
b) Dip bread into egg mixture, coating each side.
c) Press both sides of bread into graham cracker crumbs.
d) Melt about 1/2 tablespoon of butter on a griddle or nonstick pan for each slice of bread.
e) Cook until brown and crispy, then flip to other side, adding a little more butter to pan first.
f) While still hot, stack the slices of French toast, layering marshmallows and Toblerone chocolate in between.
g) Cut in half for 2 servings.

9. Ambrosia Crêpes

Makes: 1 Serving

INGREDIENTS:
- 4 Crêpes
- 16-ounce can fruit cocktail
- 1 can Frozen dessert topping - thawed
- 1 small Ripe banana sliced
- ½ cup Miniature marshmallows
- ⅓ cup Shredded coconut

INSTRUCTIONS:
a) Garnish with additional topping and fruit.
b) To freeze Crêpes stack with waxed paper between.
c) Wrap in heavy foil or freezer paper.
d) Heat in a 350° oven for 10-15 minutes.

SNACKS AND APPETIZERS

10. Sweet potato Marshmallow bites

Makes: 6-8

INGREDIENTS:
- 4 sweet potatoes, peeled and sliced
- 2 tablespoons melted plant-based butter
- 1 teaspoon maple syrup
- Kosher salt
- 10-ounce bag of marshmallows
- ½ cup of pecan halves

INSTRUCTIONS:
a) Preheat the oven to 400 degrees Fahrenheit.
b) Toss sweet potatoes with melted plant-based butter and maple syrup on a baking sheet and arrange them in an even layer. Season with salt and pepper.
c) Bake until soft, about 20 minutes, flipping halfway through. Remove.
d) Top each sweet potato round with a marshmallow and broil for 5 minutes.
e) Serve immediately with a pecan half on top of each marshmallow.

11. Rocky Road Bites

Makes: 24

INGREDIENTS:
- 350g chocolate chips
- 30g butter
- 397g tin condensed sweetened milk
- 365g dry-roasted peanuts
- 500g white marshmallows, chopped

INSTRUCTIONS:
a) Line a 9x13-inch tin with greaseproof paper.
b) In a microwave-safe bowl, microwave chocolate and butter until melted.
c) Stir occasionally until the chocolate is smooth. Stir in condensed milk.
d) Combine peanuts and marshmallows; stir into chocolate mixture.
e) Pour into prepared tin and chill until firm. Cut into squares.

12. <u>Baked Candy Apple Surprise</u>

Makes: 4 servings

INGREDIENTS:
- 4 Red Apples, cored halfway through and peeled
- ⅓ down from the top 16 red hot candy pieces
- 8 miniature marshmallows

INSTRUCTIONS:
a) Add apples to a microwave-safe casserole dish.
b) Place a candy, then a marshmallow in the center of each apple.
c) Cover the dish with plastic wrap or waxed paper.
d) Microwave for 7 minutes.
e) Add another layer of candy and marshmallows.
f) Cover and cook again for 5 minutes.

13. S'mores on the grill

Makes: 4 Servings

INGREDIENTS:
- A handful of dark chocolate candy bars
- Handful M and M's
- A handful of Peanut butter cups
- Handful Graham crackers
- Handful Chocolate
- Handful Marshmallows

INSTRUCTIONS:
a) Preheat the grill to a medium setting.
b) On a flat surface, place a 10" by 12" piece of foil.
c) Crumble a graham cracker and place it on the foil.
d) Place your chosen candy on the graham cracker, then top it with the marshmallows of your choice.
e) Wrap lightly in foil and top with the remaining graham cracker crumbs.
f) Heat for 2 to 3 minutes on the grill, or until the marshmallow has melted.

14. Chilled Fruity Treat

Makes: 4 servings

INGREDIENTS:
- 18 ounces package of refrigerated sugar cookie dough
- 7 ounces jar marshmallow crème
- 8 ounces package of cream cheese, softened

INSTRUCTIONS:
a) Set your oven to 350 degrees F before doing anything else.
b) Place the dough on a medium baking sheet about ¼-inch thick.
c) Cook everything in the oven for about 10 minutes.
d) Remove everything from the oven and keep it aside to cool.
e) In a bowl, mix the cream cheese and marshmallow crème.
f) Spread the cream cheese mixture over the crust and refrigerate to chill before serving.

15. <u>Banana Boat</u>

Makes: 4 servings

INGREDIENTS:
- 1 Banana
- Raisins
- Mini marshmallows
- Brown sugar
- Chocolate chips

INSTRUCTIONS:
a) Partially peel the banana. Cut wedge-shaped section in banana. Remove wedge.
b) Place in hollow: marshmallows, chocolate chips, and raisins,
c) Sprinkle lightly with brown sugar.
d) Cover mixture with banana peel and wrap in foil.
e) Place in coals for about 5 minutes, until chocolate and marshmallows are melted.

16. <u>Chocolate Marshmallow Blondies</u>

Makes: 10 servings

INGREDIENTS:
- ¾ cup white rice flour
- ½ cup potato starch
- ½ cup arrowroot powder
- ½ teaspoon xanthan gum
- 1 tablespoon unsweetened cocoa powder
- 1 teaspoon baking powder
- ½ teaspoon salt
- ½ cup unsalted butter softened
- ¾ cup white sugar
- ¾ cup light brown sugar, packed
- 2 large eggs
- 2 teaspoons vanilla extract
- 1 cup mini marshmallows
- ½ cup mini chocolate chips

INSTRUCTIONS:
a) Preheat the oven to 180C / 350F and grease a 9x13-inch baking pan.
b) Combine the rice flour, arrowroot powder, cornstarch, cocoa powder, xanthan gum, baking powder, and salt in a mixing bowl.
c) In a separate bowl, add sugar and butter and whisk until fluffy and light.
d) Add the eggs and vanilla extract and beat until smooth.
e) Beat in the dry **INGREDIENTS:** in small batches until smooth and well combined.
f) Fold in the chocolate chips and marshmallows then spread the batter in the prepared pan.
g) Bake for 25 to 28 minutes until the blondies are set.
h) Let the blondies cool completely before cutting into bars.

17. Birthday Sprinkles Rice Krispies Treats

Makes: 4 servings

INGREDIENTS:
- 5 cups Rice Krispies
- 3 tablespoons butter
- 4 cups-PUFFED Miniature Marshmallows
- Pinch of salt
- 1 teaspoon vanilla extract
- ½ cup sprinkles
- 2 Tablespoons neutral oil
- 1½ cups white chocolate
- Blue gel drop

INSTRUCTIONS:
a) Spray an 8x8 inch baking pan with cooking spray and set aside.
b) In a large saucepan, melt butter, vanilla extract, and salt over low heat. Add marshmallows and stir until just melted and smooth.
c) Remove from heat and stir in Rice Krispies and ½ cup sprinkles. Stir until well-coated.
d) Spray a large spatula with cooking spray and use it to press the mixture evenly into the prepared pan.
e) To make white chocolate topping: Melt white chocolate with ¼ cup of condensed milk in a medium saucepan over low heat. Once melted, add in remove and1 or 2 drops of blue food coloring, depending on how intense you'd like the color. pour over rice Krispies.

18. Biscuits with marshmallow

Makes: 12 bars

INGREDIENTS:
- ½ cup butter
- 1 ½ cups graham cracker crumbs
- 14-ounce can of sweetened condensed milk
- 2 cups semisweet chocolate chips
- 1 cup peanut butter chips ½ cup candy corn

INSTRUCTIONS:
a) Preheat oven to 325 degrees F.
b) Place butter in a 9- x 13-inch baking dish and place in oven just until butter melts.
c) Remove the dish from the oven and distribute melted butter evenly over the bottom.
d) Sprinkle graham cracker crumbs evenly over melted butter; pour sweetened condensed milk evenly over crumbs.
e) Top with chocolate chips and peanut butter chips; press down firmly.
f) Bake for 25 to 30 minutes, until golden.
g) Remove from oven; immediately sprinkle with candy corn and gently press candies into uncut bars. Cool then cut into bars.

19. Cranberry Popcorn Bars

Makes: 4 servings

INGREDIENTS:
- 3 ounces microwave popcorn, popped
- ¾ cup white chocolate chips
- ¾ cup sweetened dried cranberries
- ½ cup sweetened flaked coconut
- ½ cup slivered almonds, coarsely chopped
- 10 ounces marshmallows
- 3 Tablespoons butter

INSTRUCTIONS:
a) Line a 13"x9" baking pan with aluminum foil; spray with non-stick vegetable spray and set aside. In a large bowl, toss together popcorn, chocolate chips, cranberries, coconut, and almonds; set aside. In a saucepan over medium heat, stir marshmallows and butter until melted and smooth.
b) Pour over popcorn mixture and toss to coat completely; quickly transfer to prepared pan.
c) Lay a sheet of wax paper over top; press down firmly. Chill for 30 minutes, or until firm. Lift bars from pan, using foil as handles; peel off foil and wax paper. Slice into bars; chill an additional 30 minutes.

20. Corny Crispy Rice Treats

Makes: 2 dozen

INGREDIENTS:
- ½ cup butter
- 9 cups mini marshmallows
- 10 cups crispy rice cereal
- 1 cup candy corn
- 1 cup Indian candy corn
- ¾ cup mini semi-sweet chocolate chips
- 2 drops yellow and 1 drop red food coloring
- 20 candy pumpkins

INSTRUCTIONS:
a) Melt together butter and marshmallows in a large saucepan over medium heat; stir until smooth. In a large bowl, combine cereal, candy corn, and chocolate chips.
b) Blend food coloring into the marshmallow mixture, adding more coloring if necessary to reach the desired shade of orange. Add marshmallow mixture to cereal mixture; stir quickly to combine.
c) Spread in a buttered 13"x9" baking pan; press with buttered hands. While still warm, press on candy pumpkins spaced 1-½ to 2 inches apart.
d) Refrigerate for one hour, or until firm; cut into squares. To make thinner treats, use a 15"x10" jelly-roll pan.

21. Candy Corn Popcorn Balls

Makes: 10

INGREDIENTS:
- 8 cups popped popcorn
- 1 cup candy corn
- ¼ cup butter
- ¼ teaspoon salt
- 10-ounces pkg. marshmallows

INSTRUCTIONS:
a) Combine popcorn and candy corn in a large bowl; set aside. Melt butter in a large saucepan over medium heat; stir in salt and marshmallows.
b) Reduce heat to low and cook, stirring frequently, for 7 minutes or until marshmallows melt and the mixture is smooth.
c) Pour over popcorn mixture, stirring to coat. Lightly coat hands with vegetable spray and shape the popcorn mixture into 4-inch balls.
d) Wrap balls individually in cellophane, if desired.

22. <u>Marshmallow Puffs</u>

Makes: 4 servings

INGREDIENTS:
- 1 tube crescent rolls
- 8 marshmallows
- 3 tablespoons butter, melted
- 3 tablespoons sugar
- 1 teaspoon cinnamon

INSTRUCTIONS:
a) Preheat oven to 375 degrees F. Grease 8 muffin cups.
b) In a small bowl, melt butter.
c) In another small bowl, combine cinnamon and sugar.
d) Roll marshmallow in melted butter; then roll in a cinnamon-sugar mixture. Wrap in a crescent roll triangle, being sure to seal tightly.
e) Place them in a prepared pan. Bake for 8-10 minutes until golden brown.

23. No-Bake Oreo Bars

Makes: 9 large bars

INGREDIENTS:
- 16 ounces double stuffed Oreos, roughly chopped
- 10.5 ounces mini marshmallows
- 4 tablespoons salted butter, room temperature

INSTRUCTIONS:
a) Spray an 8×8-inch baking dish with nonstick cooking spray or line it with parchment paper. Set aside.
b) In a large microwave-safe bowl, combine marshmallows and butter.
c) Melt the marshmallows and butter in the microwave in 30-second intervals, stirring in between, until melted, about 2 minutes.
d) Add chopped Oreos to the marshmallow mixture and stir.
e) Pour mixture into the prepared 8×8-inch pan and press into the pan with a spatula.
f) Top with reserved chopped Oreo cookies.
g) Place pan in the refrigerator to set for at least 2 hours, up to overnight.

24. Strawberry Rice Krispie Oreo Treats

Makes: 18

INGREDIENTS:
- 4 cups Rice Krispies Cereal
- 3 cups mini marshmallows
- ¼ cup infused butter
- 1 box Strawberry Jell-o
- 2 cups of Chopped Golden Oreos

INSTRUCTIONS:
a) Line an 8x8 square pan with foil and lightly spray with cooking spray. Set aside.
b) In a 3 quart pan, melt the cannabis-infused butter and marshmallows over medium heat.
c) Stir in the Jell-O mix.
d) Stir until blended then fold in Rice Krispies and Golden Oreos.
e) Press mixture into prepared pan.
f) Let cool for at least 2 hours before cutting into bars and serving.

25. Oreo pizza

Makes: 8 Servings

INGREDIENTS:
- 21-ounce reduced-fat brownie mix
- 1½ cups Reduced Fat Oreo cookie crumbs
- 1 cup miniature marshmallows
- ¼ cup walnuts, chopped
- ¼ cup Reese's Pieces peanut butter candy

INSTRUCTIONS:
a) Preheat oven to 350, Prepare a 14" pizza pan with cooking spray and set aside.
b) Prepare brownie mix batter according to package directions, stir in cookie crumbs.
c) Spread batter in prepared pan. Bake for 18 minutes or until done.
d) Sprinkle marshmallows over top of the hot brownie.
e) Bake for 3 minutes more or until marshmallows is lightly browned.
f) Sprinkle with nuts and candy, pressing lightly into softened marshmallows.
g) Cool slightly on the wire rack.

26. Marshmallow Oreo Treats

Makes: 20

INGREDIENTS:
- 9 cups Oreo crushed
- 8 tablespoons salted butter
- 10 cups mini marshmallows divided

INSTRUCTIONS:
a) Line a 9×13-inch baking pan with parchment paper and set aside.
b) Add Oreos to a large Ziploc bag and use a rolling pin to crush them, set aside.
c) In a large pot, melt the butter and 8 cups of marshmallows over low heat until smooth.
d) Remove from heat and add the crushed Oreos and the marshmallows to the pot and stir until evenly coated.
e) Transfer the mixture to the baking dish and gently press the mixture into the pan.
f) Allow them to sit at room temperature for at least 1 hour before slicing.

27. Mini Oreo magical pizza

Makes: 8 servings

INGREDIENTS:
- 1 pack 7.5 oz Mini Oreo Cookies
- 1 pack 16 oz brownie mix
- 1 cup Miniature marshmallows
- ⅓ cup Chopped walnuts
- ⅓ cup Candy coated peanut butter candies

INSTRUCTIONS:
a) Reserve 20 cookies. Prepare brownie mix according to package directions. Stir in remaining cookies.
b) Spread batter in a greased 12" pizza pan. Bake at 350F for 18-20 minutes or until done.
c) Sprinkle marshmallows over the top of the hot brownie; bake for 3-5 minutes more or until marshmallows are lightly browned.
d) Sprinkle with nuts, candies and remaining cookies, pressing lightly into the softened marshmallows.
e) Cool slightly on wire rack. Cut into wedges; serve warm or cool.

28. Oreo cookie dessert (grasshopper pie)

Makes: 6 Servings

INGREDIENTS:
- 2½ cup Miniature Marshmallows
- 4 ounces Butter
- ½ cup Milk
- 3 tablespoons Creme de menthe
- 1 cup Whipped Cream (no sugar)
- 14 Oreo cookies, crushed in blender

INSTRUCTIONS:
a) Heat Marshmallows in milk until dissolved - cool slightly, add Creme De Menthe.
b) Cool well Fold in whipped cream.
c) Mix butter with crumbs and press in 9X9 pan, pour filling in top with a few crumbs and chill.

29. Sweet Potato Marshmallow Casserole

Makes: 10 Servings

INGREDIENTS:
- 4 ½ pounds sweet potatoes
- 1 cup granulated sugar
- ½ cup vegan butter softened
- ¼ cup plant-based milk
- 1 teaspoon vanilla extract
- ¼ teaspoon salt
- 1 ¼ cups cornflakes cereal, crushed
- ¼ cup chopped pecans
- 1 tablespoon brown sugar
- 1 tablespoon vegan butter, melted
- 1½ cups miniature marshmallows

INSTRUCTIONS:
a) Preheat the oven to 425 degrees Fahrenheit.
b) Roast sweet potatoes for 1 hour or until soft.
c) Slice sweet potatoes in half and scoop out the insides into a mixing dish.
d) Using an electric mixer, beat the mashed sweet potatoes, granulated sugar, and the following 5 ingredients until smooth.
e) Spoon the potato mixture into an 11 x 7-inch baking dish that has been greased.
f) In a mixing bowl, combine cornflakes cereal and the next three ingredients.
g) Sprinkle in diagonal rows 2 inches apart over the dish.
h) Bake for 30 minutes.
i) In between rows of cornflakes, sprinkle marshmallows; bake for 10 minutes.

30. Yuzu Cereal Treats

Makes: 12 bars

INGREDIENTS:
- 6 cups Rice Krispy Cereal
- 16-ounce package of mini marshmallows
- 4 tablespoons salted butter
- ¾ teaspoon yuzu extract
- Sprinkles

INSTRUCTIONS:
a) In a large pot, melt butter and 7 cups of mini marshmallows on medium heat.
b) Make sure you stir every 15-30 seconds until the two **INGREDIENTS:** are combined.
c) Mix in a few drops of yuzu extract.
d) Add in Rice Krispy cereal and mix until everything is coated in the marshmallow mixture.
e) Let sit for 1 minute to cool.
f) Add remaining marshmallows 1 cup at a time. Stir after each addition.
g) Spray a 9x13" pan with non-stick cooking spray and then pour the mixture into the pan.
h) Spray non-stick cooking spray on your hands and press the mixture down into the pan.
i) Add sprinkles all over the top and lightly press down.
j) Place in the refrigerator for at least 30 minutes.
k) Once the treats and cooled, cut them into individual servings.

31. Cranberry Popcorn Bars

Makes: 4 servings

INGREDIENTS:
- 3 ounces microwave popcorn, popped
- ¾ cup white chocolate chips
- ¾ cup sweetened dried cranberries
- ½ cup sweetened flaked coconut
- ½ cup slivered almonds, coarsely chopped
- 10 ounces marshmallows
- 3 Tablespoons butter

INSTRUCTIONS:
a) Line a 13 inchx9 inch baking pan with aluminum foil; spray with non-stick vegetable spray and set aside. In a large bowl, toss together popcorn, chocolate chips, cranberries, coconut, and almonds; set aside. In a saucepan over medium heat, stir marshmallows and butter until melted and smooth.
b) Pour over popcorn mixture and toss to coat completely; quickly transfer to prepared pan.
c) Lay a sheet of wax paper over top; press down firmly. Chill for 30 minutes, or until firm. Lift bars from pan, using foil as handles; peel off foil and wax paper. Slice into bars; chill an additional 30 minutes.

32. Candy Corn Popcorn Balls

Makes: 10

INGREDIENTS:
- 8 cups popped popcorn
- 1 cup candy corn
- ¼ cup butter
- ¼ teaspoon salt
- 10-ounces pkg. marshmallows

INSTRUCTIONS:
a) Combine popcorn and candy corn in a large bowl; set aside. Melt butter in a large saucepan over medium heat; stir in salt and marshmallows.
b) Reduce heat to low and cook, stirring frequently, for 7 minutes or until marshmallows melt and the mixture is smooth.
c) Pour over popcorn mixture, stirring to coat. Lightly coat hands with vegetable spray and shape the popcorn mixture into 4-inch balls.
d) Wrap balls individually in cellophane, if desired.

33. <u>Marshmallow Popcorn Milkshake</u>

Makes: 2 servings

INGREDIENTS:
- 1 cup whole milk
- ⅔ cup popcorn
- ½ cup mini marshmallows
- ⅔ cup vanilla ice cream
- ¼ teaspoon salt

INSTRUCTIONS:
a) Place the popcorn in a blender and pulse until the popcorn becomes like a fine breadcrumb.
b) Then add the marshmallows, milk, and ice cream. Blend until smooth.
c) Taste the milkshake and see how tastes first without the added salt.
d) Then add the marshmallows, milk, and ice cream. Blend until smooth.
e) Taste the milkshake and see how tastes first without the added salt.

34. <u>Chocolate Glazed Popcorn Squares</u>

INGREDIENTS:

- 1 pk Microwave popcorn popped
- 2 tablespoons Butter
- 10 ½ ounces Mini marshmallows
- ¼ cup Chocolate ready-to-spread - frosting
- ½ cup Salted peanuts
- ⅓ c Chocolate ready-to-spread - frosting

INSTRUCTIONS:

a) Grease 9x13 inch pan.
b) Remove and discard unpopped kernels from popcorn.
c) Place butter in 4-quarts microwavable bowl.
d) Microwave, uncovered, on HIGH, for about 30 seconds, or until melted.
e) Stir in marshmallows and frosting until marshmallows are coated.
f) Microwave, uncovered, 2-3 minutes, stirring every minutes, just until mixture is smooth.
g) Fold in peanuts and popcorn until coated.
h) Press mixture into pan.
i) Spread with chocolate glaze; cool.
j) Cut into bars.
k) CHOCOLATE GLAZE: Place ready to spread frosting in small microwavable bowl.
l) Microwave, on HIGH, about 30 seconds or until just melted.

35. Heavenly Hash Popcorn

INGREDIENTS:

- ¼ cup Butter
- 1 cup Chocolate chips
- 1 cup Pecans toasted
- 6 cups Popcorn popped
- 4 cups Miniature marshmallows

INSTRUCTIONS:

a) In a heavy saucepan, put the butter, chocolate and pecans.
b) Cook over a moderate heat until melted, stirring frequently to prevent burning. Pour over the popped corn and marshmallows.
c) Stir well. Spread on a buttered cookie sheet and refrigerate to cool.
d) For variations, you may wish to substitute butterscotch morsels or use bitter chocolate. White chocolate pieces in place of chips make a pretty white candy which can be colored and molded into shaped cake pans. Yogurt candy coating can also be used for a more piquant flavor.

36. Jelly Bean Popcorn Heaven

INGREDIENTS:

- 6 - 8 cups popcorn
- 1 jar (7 ounces) marshmallow cream
- ½ cup peanut butter
- 1 cup small jelly beans

INSTRUCTIONS:

a) Mix marshmallow cream and peanut butter in a large bowl.

b) Stir in popcorn and jelly beans until coated evenly.

c) Press mixture into greased 9-inch square baking pan.

d) Refrigerate until set, about 4 hours. Cut into squares.

37. LolliPopCorn Surprise

INGREDIENTS:
- 7 c Popped corn
- 3 c Miniature marshmallows
- 2 tablespoons Butter
- ¼ teaspoon Salt
- Food color
- 8 Lollipops

INSTRUCTIONS:
a) Measure popped corn into large, buttered bowl.
b) Heat marshmallows, butter, and salt over low heat, stirring often, until melted and smooth.
c) Add food color.
d) Pour over popped corn and toss gently.
e) Shape around lollipops into 3 inch balls.

38. Marshmallow Creme Popcorn

INGREDIENTS:
- 8 Cups popped popcorn
- 1 cup puffed rice cereal
- 3 Tablespoons butter
- 7-ounces jar marshmallow creme

INSTRUCTIONS:

a) Combine popcorn and cereal in large, greased bowl. Melt butter in medium saucepan over low heat. Remove from heat. Stir in marshmallow creme. Pour over popcorn mixture. Stir to coat evenly. Press mixture into greased 9-inch square baking pan. Refrigerate until firm, about four hours. Cut into bars.

39. Black Forest Wine Rice Crispy Treats

Makes 16 bars

INGREDIENTS:
- 3 tablespoons butter
- 4 cups mini-marshmallows
- 1/2 cup Pennsylvania cherry wine
- 5 cups puffed rice cereal
- 1/2 cup chopped dried cherries
- 1/4 cup semisweet chocolate chips

INSTRUCTIONS:
a) Line a baking sheet with parchment paper. Spray with cooking oil.
b) In a medium saucepan over medium heat, melt butter. Add marshmallows and stir until melted.
c) Remove from heat and add wine and cereal. Mix until just combined and marshmallow is distributed.
d) Add dried cherries and chocolate chips and mix until fully incorporated. Pour into prepared sheet pan, cover with parchment and chill. Slice and serve.

40. Ube Rice Krispies Treats

Makes: 8 treats

INGREDIENTS:
- ½ cup unsalted butter
- 10 ounces marshmallows
- 6 cups rice krispies
- 1 teaspoon ube extract
- 1 cup ube halaya

INSTRUCTIONS:
a) Evenly split the butter, marshmallows, and rice krispies into three batches and work with one batch at a time. Spread a thin layer of butter all over a 8.25" W x 5" D baking dish.
b) For the first batch - melt the butter in a pot on low heat, and then add in 1 batch of the marshmallows.
c) Once fully melted, add in 3-4 drops of the ube extract and stir.
d) Pour in 2 cups of the rice krispies and mix together.
e) Dump out the mixture into the baking dish and press firmly to create a flat layer.
f) For the second and third batch - repeat as step 2, adding a few more drops of ube extract for each batch.
g) Allow the rice krispie treats to fully cool and set. Spread the ube halaya on the top and cut into 8 pieces.

41. Toblerone Hot Cocoa Bombs

INGREDIENTS:
- 2 cups Chocolate Candy Melts
- 2 cups Hot Chocolate Mix
- 2 cups Mini Marshmallows
- 1 Toblerone Bar, broken into triangles

INSTRUCTIONS

a) Place chocolate candy melts in a microwave safe bowl and melt in the microwave per the directions on the package.

b) Place 1 tbsp melted candy melt into one half of a bomb mold and, using the bottom of your tablespoon measuring spoon, press the chocolate up the sides of the mold, keeping it thick but even. Repeat with 12 bomb mold halves.

c) Place the chocolate filled bomb molds into the freezer for 5 minutes.

d) Remove molds from the freezer and gently tap the sides of the mold, pressing on one side of the chocolate to make the chocolate slide out of the mold.

e) Fill 6 of the molds with 1 tbsp hot chocolate mix, 1 triangle of Toblerone candy and 6-8 mini marshmallows.

f) Heat a plate or a flat-bottom bowl in the microwave until the surface of the plate is warm to the touch. Press one of the empty chocolate bomb halves open-side-down onto the flat portion of the warm plate for about 10 seconds. This will gently melt the rim of the chocolate cup. Immediately press this warmed edge chocolate cup to the top of one of the filled cups. This will join the two halves of the hot cocoa bomb. Alternatively, you can pipe a little chocolate on the rim's edge.

g) Using a piping bag or a fork, place a tsp of the remaining chocolate candy melts on top of the assembled hot cocoa bombs then immediately follow by placing an additional triangle piece of Toblerone candy bar on this chocolate dab.

h) Place the hot cocoa bombs into the freezer for 5 minutes to get them to set, then remove and store in an airtight container until you're ready to use.

i) To use the hot cocoa bombs, place them in a mug and pour 2 cups hot milk over the top. Stir until the hot cocoa bombs are completely melted and enjoy!

42. <u>Chocolate Toblerone Dip</u>

INGREDIENTS:

- 200g Toblerone chocolate, blocks separated
- 400 g thickened cream
- 1 tablespoon honey
- Fruit, marshmallows, banana lollies serve

INSTRUCTIONS

a) Whip cream until soft peaks form, do not over whip.
b) Melt toblerone, either in microwave on 50% for 1 minute, stir, again for another 30 seconds, mix, repeat until completely melted or over boiling water on stove top.
c) Stir in the honey.
d) Gently fold the chocolate through the whipped cream.
e) Keep in refrigerator until ready to serve.
f) Serve with fruit, marshmallows or banana lollies.

43. Rice Krispie Toblerone Chewies

INGREDIENTS:
BOTTOM LAYER
- 1/2 cup corn syrup
- 1/2 cup brown sugar
- 1/2 cup peanut butter
- 1/4 cup butter
- 7 cups mini marshmallows
- 2 mini Toblerone bars, chopped
- 6 cups Rice Krispies

MIDDLE LAYER
- 8 ounces brick cream cheese, softened
- 1 cup crunchy peanut butter
- 1/2 cup icing sugar

TOP LAYER
- 4 mini Toblerone bars, chopped

INSTRUCTIONS:

a) Spray a 9 x 13 pan with cooking spray. Set aside.

b) Bottom layer - In a large pot, place corn syrup, brown sugar, peanut butter over medium-low heat.

c) Stir until melted. Add butter, mini marshmallows, and 2 Toblerone bars and stir until melted.

d) Remove from heat and stir in Rice Krispies.

e) Working fairly quickly - it sets as it cools - scrape mixture into prepared pan.

f) Spray your hands with cooking spray and pat mixture down. Set aside.

g) Middle layer - Put cream cheese and peanut butter into a microwave safe bowl.

h) Microwave for 30 - 40 seconds, until starts to get melty and is easy to stir together.

i) Stir in icing sugar. Spread evenly over the Rice Krispies.

j) Top layer - put remaining Toblerone bars into a microwave safe bowl.

k) Heat in 20 second increments until melted. Stir until smooth.

l) Pour over cream cheese layer and gently spread out evenly over bar.

m) Let chill until chocolate has firmed up.

n) Cut and serve. You don't have to keep chilled; room temp is fine.

44. <u>Marshmallow treats</u>

Makes: 24 treats

INGREDIENTS:
- 10 ounces Marshmallows
- 6 cups Rice Krispie
- 3 tablespoons sprinkles

INSTRUCTIONS:
a) Melt marshmallows over low heat or in microwave.
b) Add butter sprinkles and stir well.
c) Add cereal and stir well quickly.
d) Press into 9" x 13" pan coated with cooking spray.

45. Smores Casserole

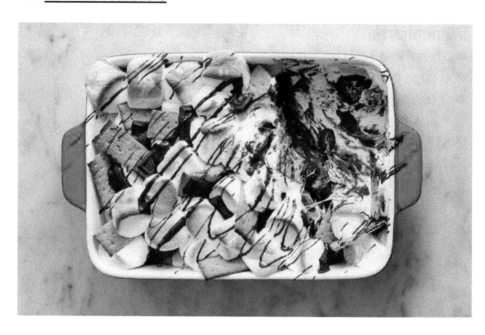

Makes: 8 servings

INGREDIENTS:
- 2 sheets frozen puff pastry, thawed
- 1 pound cream cheese, softened
- 1 cup granulated sugar
- 7 ounces jar marshmallow creme
- 9 graham crackers
- 6 tbs. melted unsalted butter
- 1 cup semisweet chocolate chips
- 2 cups miniature marshmallows

INSTRUCTIONS:

a) Preheat the oven to 375°. Lightly spray a 9 x 13 baking pan with non-stick cooking spray. Roll 1 sheet puff pastry large enough to fit the bottom of the baking pan. Place the puff pastry in the bottom of the pan. Prick the puff pastry all over with a fork.

b) Bake for 4 minutes. Remove from the oven and cool completely before filling.

c) In a mixing bowl, add the cream cheese and ¾ cup granulated sugar. Using a mixer on medium speed, beat until smooth and combined. Add the marshmallow creme to the bowl. Mix until combined and spread over the puff pastry in the pan.

d) Crush the graham crackers into crumbs in a small bowl. Add 2 tablespoons granulated sugar and 3 tablespoons butter to the bowl. Stir until combined and sprinkle over the top of the cream filling.

e) Sprinkle the chocolate chips and miniature marshmallows over the top. Roll the second sheet of puff pastry large enough to cover the top.

f) Prick the pastry all over with a fork and place over the top of the casserole. Brush 3 tablespoons butter over the top of the puff pastry. Sprinkle the remaining granulated sugar over the top.

g) Bake for 12-15 minutes or until the puff pastry is puffed and golden brown.

h) Remove from the oven and cool for 5 minutes before serving.

46. Nutella Smores

Makes: 4-6 servings

INGREDIENTS:
- 4 whole graham crackers, broken into two square halves
- 2 tablespoons Nutella
- 2 tablespoons marshmallow cream

INSTRUCTIONS:
a) Put half a teaspoon of hazelnut spread over four graham cracker halves and half teaspoon marshmallow cream over the remaining 3 cracker halves.
b) Now take one marshmallow half, and one hazelnut spread topped half, and press together.
c) Do this for all crackers to get multiple sets and serve.

47. <u>Chocolate-Cinnamon Dip</u>

Makes: 6

INGREDIENTS:
- 1 (8 ounce) package cream cheese, softened
- 1 (7 ounce) jar marshmallow creme
- 1 (12 ounce) container frozen whipped topping, thawed
- 1 teaspoon ground cinnamon
- ½ teaspoon vanilla extract
- 2 ½ tablespoons Nutella, such as Nutella

INSTRUCTIONS:
a) Take out a large bowl and mix cream cheese, whipped topping and marshmallow cream in a blender.
b) Now add cinnamon, chocolate spread and vanilla and continuing mixing.
c) Cover this dip with plastic wrap in a serving dish before refrigerating for one hour.
d) Enjoy.

48. Strawberry Nutella Bark

Makes: 45

INGREDIENTS:
- 3 Cups strawberries, stemmed and quartered
- 4 Cups dark chocolate chips, melted
- 3 Cups peanut butter, melted
- 3 Cups Nutella, melted
- 2 Cups marshmallow cream, melted

INSTRUCTIONS:
a) Cover a cookie sheet with parchment paper.
b) Get a bowl and add in your strawberries.
c) Grab a potato masher and puree the strawberries.
d) Combine in: marshmallow cream, melted chocolate, hazelnut spread, and peanut butter.
e) Now pour this mix onto your cookie sheet.
f) Place the contents in the fridge for 60 mins.
g) Enjoy.

49. Brownie Bars

Makes: 8

INGREDIENTS:
Brownie:
- ½ cup butter, cubed
- 1 ounce unsweetened chocolate
- 2 large eggs, beaten
- 1 teaspoon vanilla extract
- 1 cup sugar
- 1 cup all-purpose flour
- 1 teaspoon baking powder
- 1 cup walnuts, chopped

Filling:
- 6 ounces cream cheese softened
- ½ cup sugar
- ¼ cup butter, softened
- 2 tablespoons all-purpose flour
- 1 large egg, beaten
- ½ teaspoon vanilla extract

Topping:
- 1 cup chocolate chips
- 1 cup walnuts, chopped
- 2 cups mini marshmallows

Frosting:
- ¼ cup butter
- ¼ cup milk
- 2 ounces cream cheese
- 1 ounce unsweetened chocolate
- 3 cups confectioners' sugar
- 1 teaspoon vanilla extract

INSTRUCTIONS:

a) In a small bowl, add and whisk all the **INGREDIENTS:** for filling until smooth.

b) Melt butter with chocolate in a large saucepan over medium heat.

c) Mix well, then remove the melted chocolate from the heat.

d) Now stir in vanilla, eggs, baking powder, flour, sugar, and nuts then mix well.

e) Spread this chocolate batter in the SearPlate.

f) Drizzle nuts, marshmallows, and chocolate chips over the batter.

g) Transfer the SearPlate to Digital Air Fryer Oven and close the door.

h) Select "Air Fry" mode by rotating the dial.

i) Press the TIME/SLICES button and change the value to 28 minutes.

j) Press the TEMP/SHADE button and change the value to 350 °F.

k) Press Start/Stop to begin cooking.

l) Meanwhile, prepare the frosting by heating butter with cream cheese, chocolate and milk in a suitable saucepan over medium heat.

m) Mix well, then remove it from the heat.

n) Stir in vanilla and sugar, then mix well.

o) Pour this frosting over the brownie.

p) Allow the brownie to cool then slice into bars.

q) Serve.

50. <u>Pink Lemonade Cereal Treats</u>

Makes: 12 bars

INGREDIENTS:
- 6 cups Rice Krispy Cereal
- 16-ounce package of mini marshmallows
- 4 tablespoons salted butter
- ¾ teaspoon lemon extract
- 3 drops of Pink food colouring
- Sprinkles

INSTRUCTIONS:
a) In a large pot, melt butter and 7 cups of mini marshmallows on medium heat.
b) Make sure you stir every 15-30 seconds until the two **INGREDIENTS:** are combined.
c) Mix in a few drops of pink food colouring and lemon extract.
d) Add in Rice Krispy cereal and mix until everything is coated in the marshmallow mixture.
e) Let sit for 1 minute to cool.
f) Add remaining marshmallows 1 cup at a time. Stir after each addition.
g) Spray a 9x13" pan with non-stick cooking spray and then pour the mixture into the pan.
h) Spray non-stick cooking spray on your hands and press the mixture down into the pan.
i) Add sprinkles all over the top and lightly press down.
j) Place in the refrigerator for at least 30 minutes.
k) Once the treats and cooled, cut them into individual servings.

MAIN COURSE

51. <u>Sweet Potato Marshmallow Casserole</u>

Makes: 10 Servings

INGREDIENTS:
- 4 ½ pounds sweet potatoes
- 1 cup granulated sugar
- ½ cup vegan butter softened
- ¼ cup plant-based milk
- 1 teaspoon vanilla extract
- ¼ teaspoon salt
- 1 ¼ cups cornflakes cereal, crushed
- ¼ cup chopped pecans
- 1 tablespoon brown sugar
- 1 tablespoon vegan butter, melted
- 1½ cups miniature marshmallows

INSTRUCTIONS:
a) Preheat the oven to 425 degrees Fahrenheit.
b) Roast sweet potatoes for 1 hour or until soft.
c) Slice sweet potatoes in half and scoop out the insides into a mixing dish.
d) Using an electric mixer, beat the mashed sweet potatoes, granulated sugar, and the following 5 ingredients until smooth.
e) Spoon the potato mixture into an 11 x 7-inch baking dish that has been greased.
f) In a mixing bowl, combine cornflakes cereal and the next three ingredients.
g) Sprinkle in diagonal rows 2 inches apart over the dish.
h) Bake for 30 minutes.
i) In between rows of cornflakes, sprinkle marshmallows; bake for 10 minutes.

52. Five cups of fruit salad

Makes: 8 Serving

INGREDIENT:
- 11 ounce Can of mandarin oranges, drained
- 13½ ounce Can pineapple chunks, drained
- ½ cup Juice from pineapple
- 1½ cup Miniature marshmallows
- 2 cups Sour cream
- 3½ ounce Flaked coconut
- 1 cup Grapes/cherries for garnish

INSTRUCTIONS:
a) Combine all ingredients except garnish, and chill for several hours or overnight.
b) Serve on lettuce cups garnished with grapes or cherries.

53. Frozen fruit salad

Makes: 6 Serving

INGREDIENTS:
- 1 Envelope unflavored gelatin
- ½ cup Boiling water
- 16 ounces Can fruit cocktail in syrup
- ½ cup Mayonnaise or Miracle Whip
- 2½ cups Sweetened whipped cream

INSTRUCTIONS:
a) Fold in ¾ cup marshmallows at the same time as the whipped cream, if you like
b) Dissolve gelatin in boiling water. Cool slightly, and then stir in fruit cocktail and mayonnaise. Refrigerate for 10 minutes. Fold in whipped cream.
c) Pour into a small loaf pan or baking dish and freeze. Slice or cut into squares, and serve on lettuce.
d) Chill for a couple of hours.

54. Orange fruit salad

Makes: 12 Serving

Ingredient
- 2 cups Boiling water-divided
- 3 ounces lemon jello
- 2 cups Ice cubes, divided
- 3 ounces orange jello
- 20 ounces crush pineapple
- 2 cups Min. marshmallows
- 3 Large bananas sliced
- ½ cup Fine shredded cheddar cheese
- 1 cup Reserved pineapple juice
- ½ cup Sugar
- Egg, beaten
- 1 tablespoon Oleo
- 1 cup Whipping cream
- 2 tablespoons Cornstarch

INSTRUCTIONS:
a) Pour into a 13"x9"x2" baking pan. Refrigerate until set. Repeat with orange jello, with remaining ice and water.
b) Stir in marshmallows. Pour over the lemon layer; refrigerate until set. For the dressing, combine pineapple juice, sugar egg, cornstarch, and butter in a pan.
c) Cook over medium heat stirring constantly until thick.
d) Cover and refrigerate overnight. Next day, arrange bananas with whipped cream over jello.
e) Combine dressing with whipped cream; spread over bananas, Sprinkle with cheese.

55. Pistachio salad

Makes: 8 servings

INGREDIENTS:
- 9 ounces pk. whipped topping
- 1 pack pistachio pudding
- 1 can crushed pineapple, drained
- 1 cup miniature marshmallows

INSTRUCTIONS:
a) Fold dry pudding mix into whipped topping. add pineapple and marshmallows.
b) Refrigerate until firm.

56. Dutch Oven Meatloaf

INGREDIENTS:
- 2 pounds ground beef
- 3 onions, chopped
- 3 potatoes, with skin, ½" cube
- 2 carrots, grated
- 1 cup potato chips
- 2 large marshmallows
- ⅔ cup catsup
- 2 ounces Tabasco

INSTRUCTIONS:
a) Mash **INGREDIENTS:** together. Place in Dutch oven.
b) Put the lid on, and place over small pile of hot coals (4-5) and cover lid with additional coals (4-5).
c) Cook for approximately 30 minutes.

57. Kids fruit salad

Makes: 5 cups

INGREDIENTS:
- 17 ounces Can fruit cocktail, drained
- 1½ cup Miniature marshmallows
- 2 mediums Bananas, sliced
- 1 medium Apple, coarsely chopped
- 2 tablespoons Yuzu juice
- ¼ cup Maraschino cherries, halved
- 1½ cup Cool whip

INSTRUCTIONS:
a) Stir sliced apples and bananas in Yuzu juice to keep them from turning dark.

b) In a large bowl, combine all ingredients except the cool whip. Gently fold in cool whip.

c) Cover, and chill until served.

d) Kids dig into this - think it is the cool whip they are interested in.

58. <u>Gumdrop fruit salad</u>

Makes: 10 servings

INGREDIENTS:
- 1 cup Whipping Cream
- 2½ cups Pineapple Tidbits, drained
- 2 cups Seedless Grapes
- 2 cups Miniature Marshmallows
- ¾ cup Gumdrops, cut fine
- 4-ounce jar of Maraschino Cherries, cut
- ½ cup Chopped Pecans
- ½ cup Pineapple Juice
- ¼ cup Sugar
- 2 tablespoons Flour
- ¼ teaspoon Salt
- 3 tablespoons Yuzu Juice
- 1½ teaspoon Vinegar

INSTRUCTIONS:
a) Whip cream and stir all ingredients together. Add cooled dressing, and refrigerate overnight.
b) Blend all ingredients in a saucepan and cook until thick, stirring constantly.
c) Cool before adding to the salad.

59. Kentucky frozen fruit salad

Makes: 8 servings

INGREDIENTS:
- 2 Yuzus, juice of
- ⅛ teaspoon Salt
- ¾ cup Pineapple juice
- 4 tablespoons Sugar
- 3 Egg yolks
- 3 tablespoons Flour
- 1 can Pineapple chunks
- 1 can Seedless Royal Anne cherries
- Few cut red and green Maraschino cherries
- 1 cup Whipped cream
- Almonds, optional
- ¼ pounds Marshmallows

INSTRUCTIONS:
a) Blend Yuzu juice, salt, pineapple juice, sugar, egg yolks, and flour. Cook until thick. Cool.
b) Add pineapple chunks, cherries, and marshmallows.
c) Fold in the whipped cream.
d) Fill empty ice cube trays and freeze.
e) Slice and serve on lettuce leaves. May be prepared days ahead of servings.

60. Marshmallow Fruit cocktail

Makes: 1 serving

INGREDIENTS:
- 8 ounces of Whipped topping
- Three 15-ounce cans of fruit cocktail in heavy syrup
- 2 cups Flaked coconut
- 3 cups Mini marshmallows
- 2 cups Raisins
- 2 mediums Bananas

INSTRUCTIONS:
a) Open the cans and drain the syrup. Place the cocktail in a bowl.
b) Cut the bananas into bite-sized slices.
c) Add the other ingredients, stirring the combined mixture with each new addition.
d) Add the whipped topping last, making sure it is well mixed throughout the medley.
e) Chill for a couple of hours.

61. <u>Lemony fruit salad</u>

Makes: 1 serving

INGREDIENTS:
- 3-ounce pack of lemon instant pudding mix
- 16-ounce can fruit cocktail, juice included
- 14-ounce can of crushed pineapple, juice included
- 1 can Mandarin oranges, drained well
- 8 ounces cool whip, thawed
- 1 cup Miniature marshmallows

INSTRUCTIONS:
a) Combine everything in a large bowl. Mix well. Chill for about 24 hours before servings. If desired, put it in a sheet cake pan instead of a bowl. It can then be cut into squares for servings.
b) If desired nuts, maraschino cherries, and the coconut may also be added.

62. Grandmother's frozen fruit salad

Makes: 6 servings

INGREDIENTS:
- 1 can Fruit cocktail
- 1 can Apricot halves
- 1 can Chunk pineapple
- 4 ounces Miniature marshmallows
- 1 pack of Unflavored gelatin
- 4 ounces Maraschino cherries
- 4 ounces of soft cream cheese
- ½ cup Salad dressing
- ¾ cup Whipping cream, whipped
- Extra apricots and mint

INSTRUCTIONS:
a) Drain fruit cocktail, apricots, and pineapple. Place fruit into a large bowl. Add marshmallows. Set aside.
b) Place fruit juices into a saucepan. Stir in gelatin. Place over medium heat. Heat, stirring, until gelatin is dissolved
c) Cool slightly. Pour over fruit. Stir in diced cherries and cherry juice.
d) In a separate bowl, blend cream cheese and salad dressing.
e) Add to fruit mixture, mixing well.
f) Cover and chill until partially set. Fold in whipped cream. Transfer to a 7 1⅕-by-11-inch serving dish.
g) Cover and place in the freezer for 4 to 6 hours or overnight. Cut into squares to serve. Garnish with apricots and mint sprig.

DESSERT

63. Carnation Marshmallow fudge

Makes: 2 servings

INGREDIENTS:
- 2 tablespoons Butter or margarine
- ⅔ cup Undiluted Evaporated Milk
- 1½ cups Granulated sugar
- ¼ teaspoon Salt
- 2 cups of miniature marshmallows
- 1½ cups Semi-Sweet Chocolate Morsels
- 1 teaspoon Vanilla extract
- ½ cup Chopped pecans or walnuts

INSTRUCTIONS:
a) Butter 8-inch square pan.
b) In a pan, combine butter, evaporated milk, sugar, and salt.
c) Bring to a boil, stirring constantly.
d) Boil for 4 to 5 minutes, stirring constantly, and remove from heat.
e) Stir in marshmallows, morsels, vanilla, and nuts.
f) Stir vigorously for 1 minute or until the marshmallows melt completely.
g) Pour into pan. Cool and cut into squares. Hint For a thicker fudge, use a 7x5-inch loaf pan.

64. Funfetti cake

Makes: 12 Servings

INGREDIENTS:
- 1 pack Moist Yellow Cake Mix
- 1 pack Vanilla instant pudding mix
- 4 Eggs
- 1 cup Water
- ½ cup Crisco oil
- 1 cup Semi-sweet mini chocolate chips
- 1 cup Colored mini-marshmallows
- ⅔ cup Chocolate Layer cake frosting
- 2 tablespoons Semi-sweet mini chocolate chips

INSTRUCTIONS:
a) Preheat the oven to 350 degrees Fahrenheit.
b) Butter and flour in a 13x9x2-inch baking pan.

TO MAKE THE CAKE
c) Whisk together cake mix, pudding mix, eggs, water, and oil using an electric mixer
d) Stir in micro chocolate chips, and then pour everything into the pan.
e) Bake for 45 minutes at 350 degrees F.

FOR THE TOPPING
f) Sprinkle marshmallows evenly over the hot cake right away. Fill a microwave-safe bowl halfway with frosting.
g) Microwave for 25-30 seconds on HIGH.
h) Stir until the mixture is completely smooth.
i) Drizzle over marshmallows and cake evenly.
j) Add 2 tablespoons of chocolate chips on top.
k) Allow cooling completely.

65. Grilled pound cake s'mores

Makes: 4 Servings

INGREDIENTS:
- 1 cup semisweet chocolate morsels
- 10.75-ounce frozen pound cake, thawed
- 1 cup marshmallow cream
- Vanilla ice cream

INSTRUCTIONS:
a) Slice the cake horizontally into three layers.
b) Spread ½ cup marshmallow cream and ½ the morsels over the bottom tier on a large sheet of heavy-duty foil.
c) To ensure a secure seal, overlap the foil edges.
d) Grill for 7-20 minutes over low heat without a grill lid.

66. Cornflake marshmallow cookies

Makes: 20 Cookies

INGREDIENTS:
- 16 tablespoons butter
- 1¼ cups granulated sugar
- ¼ cup light brown sugar
- 1 egg
- ½ teaspoon vanilla extract
- 1½ cups flour
- ½ teaspoon baking powder
- ¼ teaspoon baking soda
- 1¼ teaspoons kosher salt
- 3 cups Cornflake Crunch
- ¼ cup mini chocolate chips
- 1¼ cups mini marshmallows

INSTRUCTIONS:
a) Combine the butter and sugars in the bowl of a stand mixer fitted with the paddle attachment and cream together on medium-high for 2 to 3 minutes. Scrape down the sides of the bowl, add the egg and vanilla, and beat for 7 to 8 minutes.

b) Reduce the mixer speed to low and add the flour, baking powder, baking soda, and salt. Mix just until the dough comes together, no longer than 1 minute.

c) Scrape down the sides of the bowl with a spatula.

d) Still on low speed, paddle in the cornflake crunch and mini chocolate chips just until they're incorporated, no more than 30 to 45 seconds.

e) Paddle in the mini marshmallows just until incorporated.

f) Using a 2¾-ounce ice cream scoop, portion out the dough onto a parchment-lined sheet pan. Pat the tops of the cookie dough domes flat. Wrap the sheet pan tightly in plastic wrap and refrigerate for at least 1 hour or up to 1 week.

g) Heat the oven to 375°F.

h) Arrange the chilled dough a minimum of 4 inches apart on parchment- or Silpat-lined sheet pans. Bake for 18 minutes. The cookies will puff, crackle, and spread.

i) At the 18-minute mark, the cookies should be browned on the edges and just beginning to brown toward the center.

j) Leave them in the oven for an additional minute or so if they aren't and they still seem pale and doughy on the surface.

k) Cool the cookies completely on the sheet pans before transferring them to a plate or an airtight container for storage. At room temperature, the cookies will keep fresh for 5 days; in the freezer, they will keep for 1 month.

67. Grasshopper pie

Makes: 1

INGREDIENTS:
- 1 serving Brownie Pie, prepared through step 8
- 1 serving of Mint Cheesecake Filling
- 20 g mini chocolate chips [2 tablespoons]
- 25 g mini marshmallows [½ cup]
- 1 serving Mint Glaze, warm

INSTRUCTIONS:
a) Heat the oven to 350°F.
b) Grab a sheet pan and put your pie tin of graham crust on it. Pour the mint cheesecake filling into the shell. Pour the brownie batter on top of it. Use the tip of a knife to swirl the batter and mint filling, teasing up streaks of the mint filling so they show through the brownie batter.
c) Sprinkle the mini chocolate chips into a small ring in the center of the pie, leaving the bull's-eye center empty. Sprinkle the mini marshmallows into a ring around the ring of chocolate chips.
d) Bake the pie for 25 minutes. It should puff slightly on the edges but still be jiggly in the center. The mini chocolate chips will look as if they are beginning to melt, and the mini marshmallows should be evenly tanned. Leave the pie in the oven for an additional 3 to 4 minutes if this is not the case.
e) Cool the pie completely before finishing it.
f) Make sure your glaze is still warm to the touch. Dunk the tines of a fork into the warm glaze, then dangle the fork about 1 inch above the bull's-eye center of the pie.
g) Transfer the pie to the fridge so the mint glaze firms up before serving—which will happen as soon as it's cold, about 15 minutes. Wrapped in plastic, the pie will keep fresh in the fridge for up to 1 week or in the freezer for up to 2 weeks.

68. Chocolate malt layer cake

Makes: 1

INGREDIENTS:
- 1 serving of Chocolate Cake
- 1 serving Ovaltine Soak
- 1 serving Malt Fudge Sauce, warm
- ½ serving Malted Milk Crumb
- 1 serving of Charred Marshmallows

INSTRUCTIONS:
a) Put a piece of parchment or a Silpat on the counter. Invert the cake onto it and peel off the parchment or Silpat from the bottom of the cake. Use the cake ring to stamp out 2 circles from the cake. These are your top 2 cake layers. The remaining cake "scrap" will come together to make the bottom layer of the cake.

THE BOTTOM
a) Clean the cake ring and place it in the center of a sheet pan lined with clean parchment or a Silpat. Use 1 strip of acetate to line the inside of the cake ring.
b) Put the cake scraps inside the ring and use the back of your hand to tamp the scraps together into a flat even layer.
c) Dunk a pastry brush in the Ovaltine soak and give the layer of cake a good, healthy bath of half of the soak.
d) Use the back of a spoon to spread one-fifth of the malt fudge sauce in an even layer over the cake.
e) Sprinkle half of the malted milk crumbs and one-third of the charred marshmallows evenly over the malt fudge sauce. Use the back of your hand to anchor them in place.
f) Use the back of a spoon to spread another fifth of the malt fudge sauce as evenly as possible over the crumbs and marshmallows.

THE MIDDLE

a) With your index finger, gently tuck the second strip of acetate between the cake ring and the top ¼ inch of the first strip of acetate, so that you have a clear ring of acetate 5 to 6 inches tall—high enough to support the height of the finished cake. Set a cake round on top of the sauce and repeat the process for layer 1.

THE TOP

a) Nestle the remaining cake round into the sauce. Cover the top of the cake with the remaining fudge sauce. Since it's a sauce, not a frosting, here you have no choice but to make a shiny, perfectly flat top. Garnish with the remaining charred marshmallows.

b) Transfer the sheet pan to the freezer and freeze for a minimum of 12 hours to set the cake and filling. The cake will keep in the freezer for up to 2 weeks.

c) At least 3 hours before you are ready to serve the cake, pull the sheet pan out of the freezer and, using your fingers and thumbs, pop the cake out of the cake ring. Gently peel off the acetate and transfer the cake to a platter or cake stand. Let it defrost in the fridge for a minimum of 3 hours.

d) Slice the cake into wedges and serve.

69. Charleston Cobblestone Ice Cream

Makes: ½ gallon

INGREDIENTS:
- 1 ½ ounces unsweetened baked chocolate
- 1 cup half–and–half
- ⅓ cup granulated sugar
- 1 cup whipping cream
- 6 egg yolks
- ⅓ cup granulated sugar
- ¼ cup unsalted butter softened
- 1 teaspoon vanilla extract
- 1 cup miniature marshmallows
- 1 cup toasted, chopped almonds
- 1 cup raisins
- 1 cup miniature chocolate chips

INSTRUCTIONS:
a) In a small saucepan, over low heat, melt chocolate with half and half. Stir until smooth. Set aside.
b) In a medium saucepan, combine ⅓ cup sugar and cream, and over medium heat, beat in egg yolks and the other ⅓ cup sugar until light and lemon colored. Temper the egg yolk mixture by stirring about half of the very hot cream mixture in. Pour egg mixture into a saucepan and continue cooking until thickened.
c) Remove from heat and stir in the softened butter and vanilla extract. Add the chocolate mixture and stir until quite smooth and well blended. Allow to cool, then refrigerate.
d) Before churning, add marshmallows, almonds, raisins, and chips.

70. <u>Chocolate Mallow Ice Cream</u>

Makes: 4 servings

INGREDIENTS:
- ½ cup semisweet chocolate chips
- ½ cup plus ⅔ cup heavy cream
- ¼ cup water
- 8 marshmallows, cut up

INSTRUCTIONS:
a) Combine chocolate chips, ½ cup cream, water, and marshmallows in a 2–quart saucepan. Cook and stir over low heat until the chocolate and marshmallows melt. Remove from heat; chill thoroughly.
b) Whip the ⅔ cup cream until stiff. Fold into cold chocolate mixture until well blended. Freeze in an ice cube tray; do not stir.

71. <u>Gooseberry-Marshmallow Ice Cream</u>

Makes: 4 servings

INGREDIENTS:
- 12 large white marshmallows
- ¾ cup evaporated milk
- 1 pound fresh or frozen gooseberries
- ⅓ cup granulated sugar
- ⅔ cup cream, whipped
- ¼ cup light corn syrup

INSTRUCTIONS:

a) Melt marshmallows with evaporated milk in a bowl placed over a pan of warm water, stirring until smooth. In a saucepan, cook half the gooseberries in 2 tablespoons water over gentle heat for about 5 minutes or until the skins burst and the fruit softens. Stir in sugar, then strain. Let cool.

b) Fold in whipped cream and pour into a container. Cover and freeze until firm.

c) Make a sauce by cooking the remaining gooseberries with corn syrup and 2 tablespoons water in a covered pan over a gentle heat until the fruit softens. Pass through a strainer and set aside.

d) About 45 minutes before serving, transfer the ice cream to the refrigerator. Just before serving, warm the sauce gently if necessary. Spoon ice cream between macaroons and pour sauce over.

72. Rocky road ice cream

Makes: about 1 ¾ pints

INGREDIENTS:
- ⅓ cup superfine sugar
- 2 cups whole milk, chilled
- ¼ cup unsweetened cocoa powder
- ½ milk chocolate, broken up
- 2 teaspoons pure vanilla extract
- 1 cup heavy cream, whipped and chilled
- 1 cup mini-marshmallows
- ½ cup mixed roughly chopped pecans and sliced almonds

INSTRUCTIONS:
a) Warm the sugar in a pan with half the milk, the cocoa powder, and the chocolate, stirring occasionally. When the chocolate is completely dissolved and the mixture is well blended, set aside to cool completely.
b) When cooled, stir in the vanilla and the rest of the milk. Whisk this gradually into the whipped cream.
c) Pour into an ice cream maker and process according to the directions. When almost frozen, tip the ice cream into a freezer container, and quickly stir in the marshmallows and nuts. If you do not have an ice cream maker, follow the hand-mixing **INSTRUCTIONS:** and stir in the marshmallows and nuts after whisking the ice cream for the last time. Freeze for 15 minutes before serving or until required.
d) Store in the freezer for up to 2 weeks but take out 15 minutes before serving to soften.

73. Key Lime Ice Cream

Makes: 4 servings

INGREDIENTS:
- ¾ cup granulated sugar
- 2 eggs
- ½ teaspoon grated lime peel
- 1 cup whole milk
- 1 cup miniature marshmallows
- 1 cup whipping cream
- ½ cup Key lime juice
- 3 drops of green food coloring

INSTRUCTIONS:
a) Combine sugar and eggs, mixing thoroughly. Add lime peel and milk. Cook over medium heat until slightly thickened. Remove from heat and add marshmallows, stirring until melted. Cool
b) Add Key lime juice and whipping cream to the cooled mixture.
c) Add food coloring as desired. Freeze as per the ice cream maker's directions.

74. S'mores Chocolate Mousse Cups

Makes: 4 servings

INGREDIENTS:
- 1 cup graham cracker crumbs
- 2 egg yolks
- ¼ cup sugar
- ½ cup whipping heavy cream
- ½ cup chocolate
- ¾ cup whipping heavy cream

INSTRUCTIONS:
a) Beat egg yolks in a small bowl with an electric mixer on high speed for about 3 minutes or until thick and lemon colored. Gradually beat in sugar.

b) Heat ½ cup whipping cream in a 2-quart saucepan over medium heat until hot. Gradually stir at least half of the hot whipping cream into the egg yolk mixture; stir back into hot cream in a saucepan. Cook over low heat for about 3 minutes, stirring constantly, until the mixture thickens.

c) Stir in chocolate chips until melted. Cover and refrigerate for about 2 hours, stirring occasionally, just until chilled.

d) Beat ¾ cups whipping cream in a chilled medium bowl with an electric mixer on high speed until stiff. Fold the chocolate mixture into whipped cream.

e) Pipe or spoon the mixture into serving bowls. Immediately refrigerate any remaining dessert after serving.

f) Top with marshmallow crème, and giant marshmallow - toast.

75. Frankenstein mug cake

Makes: 12 servings

INGREDIENTS:
FOR THE CUPCAKES:
- 200g soft butter
- 175g golden caster sugar
- 250g self-rising flour
- 1 teaspoon baking powder
- ¼ teaspoon salt
- 3 large eggs
- ½ teaspoon vanilla extract
- 100ml milk

TO DECORATE:
- 300g icing sugar, sifted
- 2-3 tablespoons milk
- green food coloring paste
- 36 mini marshmallows, 12 snipped in half, for the eyes

INSTRUCTIONS:

a) Heat oven to 180C/160C fan/gas 4 and line a 12-hole muffin tin with deep muffin cases. Cream the butter with the sugar until pale and fluffy. Add the remaining cake **INGREDIENTS:** and beat until smooth.

b) Spoon into the muffin cases and bake for 20 mins or until golden and a skewer inserted into one of the middle cakes comes out clean. Cool for 5 mins in the tin, then completely on a wire rack

c) Using a small, sharp serrated knife, cut a semi-circle piece of cake from the left and right of each cake, to make stepped edges, level with the cupcake case.

d) Next, make a width-ways cut about 3cm from the top of the cake, about 1cm deep. Slice a 5mm piece off the surface of the cake to meet this cut, to make a flat, raised face and prominent forehead. Chill for 10 mins to firm the crumbs

e) Mix the icing sugar, milk, and green coloring to make a very thick icing that flows slowly from the spoon. Spoon 1 tablespoon onto a cake and let it begin to spread   itself over the cut shape. Ease it here and there with a palette knife to coat it.

f) Add marshmallow neck bolts and eyes. Repeat for each cupcake.

g) Leave to set, then pipe on the faces and hair

76. Spiderweb Cake

Makes: 12

INGREDIENTS:
- 18.5-ounce box chocolate cake mix, batter prepared
- 1 cup mini marshmallows
- 16-ounce container of white frosting
- 4 drops of red food color
- 4 drops of yellow food color
- 2 black jelly beans
- 1 tube of black decorating gel or 1 string of black licorice

INSTRUCTIONS:
a) Preheat oven to 350 degrees F. Coat two 8-inch cake pans with cooking spray. Pour cake batter into pans and bake for 28 to 30 minutes, or until a toothpick inserted in the center comes out clean.

b) While still warm, invert one cake onto a serving platter. Top with mini marshmallows and place the second cake layer right-side up over the marshmallows. Let sit for 5 minutes for the marshmallows to melt then chill until firm.

c) In a small bowl, mix 1-¼ cups of white frosting with red and yellow food colors until the frosting is orange. Frost the top and sides of the cake.

d) Place the remaining white frosting into a resealable plastic storage bag. Cut a very small tip off the corner of the bag and pipe a Spiderweb design on top of the cake.

e) Place a black jelly bean on Spiderweb and draw legs with a black gel or form them with licorice to look like a spider.

f) Repeat with the remaining jelly bean and gel to form a second spider.

77. <u>Five-minute fudge</u>

Makes: 4 servings

INGREDIENTS:
- ⅔ cup Evaporated Milk
- 1⅔ cup Sugar
- ½ teaspoon Salt
- 1½ cup Marshmallows
- 1½ cups Chocolate Chips
- 1 teaspoon Vanilla

INSTRUCTIONS:
a) Combine Milk, Sugar, and Salt in a saucepan over medium heat.
b) Bring to a boil and cook for 4-5 minutes, stirring constantly. Remove from heat.
c) Add Marshmallows, Chocolate Chips, and vanilla.
d) Stir vigorously for 1 minute.
e) Pour into a buttered 8" square pan.
f) Cool until it doesn't fall out or slosh around in the pan.
g) Add ½ cup of chopped nuts before pouring them into a pan.

78. Easter egg mousse

Makes: 4 servings

INGREDIENTS:
- 8 x 25g chocolate bars
- 25g Butter
- 75g Freedom marshmallows
- 30ml Water
- ½ teaspoon Vanilla extract
- 140ml double cream

INSTRUCTIONS:
a) Melt 3 of the chocolate bars in a heatproof bowl over a pan of simmering water.
b) Remove the egg halves from the molds and put them back in the fridge.
c) Place the remaining chocolate bars, butter, marshmallows, and water into a small saucepan.
d) Cook over low heat and stir well until the mixture is a smooth texture. Remove from heat and leave to cool.
e) Add the vanilla extract to the double cream and whisk until firm peaks form
f) Gently fold the whipped double cream into the smooth chocolate mixture and divide equally between the easter egg molds.

79. Pineapple Marshmallow Ice Cream

Makes: 6 servings

INGREDIENTS:
- 1 cup miniature marshmallows
- ½ cup medium dry white wine or unsweetened apple juice
- 1 ⅔ cups canned crushed pineapple, thoroughly drained, syrup reserved
- 1 ¼ cups cream, whipped
- ¼ cup drained maraschino cherries, roughly chopped

INSTRUCTIONS:
a) Put marshmallows, wine or apple juice, and pineapple syrup in a saucepan over low heat, stirring constantly, until the marshmallows have dissolved. Let cool.
b) Fold cream into the cooled marshmallow mixture. Pour into a container, cover, and freeze to the slushy stage. Beat well in a bowl. Fold crushed pineapple and cherries into the frozen mixture. Return to the container, cover, and freeze until firm.
c) About 20 minutes before serving, transfer the ice cream to the refrigerator. Decorate each portion with pineapple cubes, maraschino cherry halves, and frosted mint leaves.

80. Caramel RumChata fondue

Makes: 12 servings

INGREDIENTS:
- 7 ounces Caramels
- ¼ cup Miniature marshmallows
- ⅓ cup Whipping cream
- 2 teaspoons RumChata

INSTRUCTIONS:
a) Combine caramels and cream in crock pot.

b) Cover and heat until melted, 30 to 60 minutes.

c) Stir in marshmallows and rumchata.

d) Cover and continue cooking for 30 minutes.

e) Serve with apple wedges or pound cake.

81. Caramel rum fondue

Makes: 12 servings

INGREDIENTS:
- 7 ounces Caramels
- ¼ cup Miniature marshmallows
- ⅓ cup Whipping cream
- 2 teaspoons Rum or 1/4 t rum extract

INSTRUCTIONS:
a) Combine caramels and cream in crock pot. Cover and heat until melted, 30 to 60 minutes.
b) Stir in marshmallows and rum.
c) Cover and continue cooking 30 minutes.
d) Serve with apple wedges or pound cake.

82. Chocolate butterscotch fondue

Makes: 1 Servings

INGREDIENTS:
- 14 ounces Sweetened condensed milk
- 6 ounces Butterscotch pieces
- 4 Squares unsweetened chocolate
- 7 ounces Marshmallow fluff
- ½ cup Milk
- 1 teaspoon Vanilla
- ½ cup Coconut; optional

INSTRUCTIONS:
a) Mix all ingredients and stir over low heat until chocolate and butterscotch melts.
b) Add milk if it becomes too thick.
c) Serve with fresh fruit. Strawberries, apple, pineapple, bananas, cherries.

83. Mocha chocolate fondue

Makes: 4 Servings

INGREDIENTS:
- 1 tablespoon Butter
- 1 Jar marshmallow creme
- ⅓ cup Coffee liqueur
- Unsweetened chocolate

INSTRUCTIONS:
a) Melt butter, chocolate and marshmallow creme together in fondue pot on high, stirring occasionally to mix. When well mixed, add coffee liqueur and stir well. Reduce heat to low for serving.

84. Toffee fondue

Makes: 1 Servings

INGREDIENTS:
- 1 pack Kraft caramels (large)
- ¼ cup Milk
- ¼ cup Strong black coffee
- ½ cup Milk chocolate chips --
- Apple wedges
- Banana chunks
- Marshmallows
- Angel food cake -- 1 inch cubes

INSTRUCTIONS:
a) Place caramels, milk, coffee and chocolate chips in top of double boiler; cook over boiling water, stirring, until melted and blended. Place in fondue pot. Spear fruits, marshmallows and cake on fondue forks; dip into fondue.

85. Tutti frutti trifle

Makes: 4 Servings

INGREDIENTS:
- ½ Grapefruit
- 1 Orange
- 1 cup Fresh pineapple
- 6 Marshmallows
- 6 Maraschino cherries
- ½ cup Moist shredded coconut
- 2 tablespoons Maraschino juice
- 3 Egg whites
- 6 tablespoons Confectioner's sugar

INSTRUCTIONS:
a) Remove segments from the membrane of grapefruit and orange, slice pineapple, and cut marshmallows and cherries into eighths. Soak marshmallows and coconut in combined juices.
b) Beat egg whites until stiff and fold in the sugar.
c) Combine with fruits and coconut marshmallow mixture. Freeze in refrigerator tray until firm.

86. Creme de menthe Parfait

Makes: 6 Servings

INGREDIENTS:
- 3 cups Miniature marshmallows
- ½ cup Milk
- 2 tablespoons Green creme de menthe
- 1 cup Semi-Sweet Chocolate Chips
- ¼ cup Powdered sugar
- 1½ cup Whipping cream
- Candy mint leaves OR- fresh mint

INSTRUCTIONS:
a) In a medium saucepan, combine marshmallows and milk. Cook over low heat, stirring constantly until the marshmallows are melted and the mixture is smooth.
b) Into a small bowl, pour 1 cup of the marshmallow mixture. Stir in creme de menthe, and set aside.
c) Add chocolate chips and powdered sugar to the marshmallow mixture remaining in the saucepan. Return the saucepan to low heat, and stir constantly until the chips are melted. Remove from heat, and cool to room temperature.
d) In a large bowl, beat whipping cream until stiff, and fold 1-½ cups into the mint mixture. Fold the remaining whipped cream into the chocolate mixture.
e) Alternately spoon chocolate and mint mixtures into parfait glasses.
f) Refrigerate until cold or place in the freezer until firm. Garnish as desired.

87. S'mores hand pies

Makes: 8 hand pies

INGREDIENTS:
- 1 pkg. (2 crusts) refrigerated uncooked piecrusts
- 2 TBSP. plus 2 tsp. butter, melted
- 1 cup marshmallow spread
- 4 double graham crackers, crumbled
- 1 cup semisweet chocolate chips
- 1 large egg, lightly beaten

INSTRUCTIONS
a) Heat the oven to 340°F (171°C).
b) Line two baking sheets with parchment paper and set aside.
c) Place piecrusts on a floured work surface and roll out slightly using a rolling pin. Using a small, overturned bowl with a 6-in. (15cm) diameter, press into dough to cut out 8 circles. Brush each circle with 1 teaspoon butter.
d) Place 2 tablespoons marshmallow spread on each circle. Equally distribute graham cracker crumbs across half of all 8 circles, leaving a ½-inch (1.25cm) rim. Top each with semisweet chocolate chips.
e) Using a pastry brush, paint edges of circles with egg. Fold over circles and press to seal. Using a fork, make indentations around crusts. With a sharp knife, make vents for steam.
f) Bake for 12 to 14 minutes or until golden brown. Allow to cool a bit before serving.
g) Storage: Keep in an airtight container at room temperature for up to 3 days.

88. Red, White and Blueberry Ice Cream

INGREDIENTS:
- 1 quart vanilla ice cream
- 1 cup chopped strawberries
- ¾ cup blueberries
- 1 cup mini marshmallows

INSTRUCTIONS

a) Scoop ice cream into a stand mixer, or large mixing bowl if you're using a hand mixer.

b) Using the paddle attachment, blend quickly until ice cream is just soft.

c) While ice cream is soft, mix in the remaining ingredients, then transfer to a container.

d) Cover and freeze until solid, about 4 hours or overnight; then serve.

89. Toblerone almond pie

Makes: 1 servings

INGREDIENTS:
- 6 Toblerone Honey and Almond Bars
- ½ cup Milk
- 1/4 lb Marshmallows
- ½ pint Heavy cream, whipped
- 1 9 inch pie shell, cooled or graham cracker shell

INSTRUCTIONS:
- Chop toblerone bars into small pieces and melt in double boiler with milk.
- Add marshmallows and stir until melted. Chill mixture thoroughly.
- Fold cream into chocolate mixture and pour into cooled pie shell.
- Chill overnight until firm.
- Top with whipped cream and serve.

90. Toblerone-Banana Party

Makes: 6 servings

INGREDIENTS:
- 5 bananas
- 2 cups of dark chocolate, melted
- 1 1/3 sticks butter
- 1 cup of flour
- 1/2 cup of sugar
- 1 eggs
- 1 toblerone
- 3 marshmallows
- 1 package of m&m's
- 1 chocolate bar
- caramel sauce

INSTRUCTIONS:
a) Peel the bananas and dig out a channel the length of each.
b) Mix the melted chocolate and butter with the flour, sugar, and eggs.
c) Pour this mixture into the casserole dish.
d) Place the bananas on top and then place pieces of Toblerone in the channel of the first banana,
e) Place halved marshmallows in the second, M&M's in the third, pieces of chocolate in the fourth, and caramel sauce in the last.
f) Bake for 20 minutes at 350 °F and enjoy hot!

91. Marshmallow Mousse

Makes 4-6

INGREDIENTS:
- 250 g marshmallows
- 200 ml half and half
- 1/2 cup Greek yogurt
- 3 drops purple food gel, optional
- 3 drops pink food gel, optional
- 3 drops orange food gel, optional

INSTRUCTIONS:
a) Over low heat, slowly cook the marshmallows and 2 tablespoons of the half & half in a small saucepan whilst stirring continuously. They can burn easily so keep an eye on them.
b) Remove from heat and continue to stir if they look like they might burn.
c) Once marshmallows have melted and the mixture is smooth, allow to cool for 5 minutes.
d) Add the remaining half and half and yogurt and mix to blend.
e) Depending on the number of layers, divide the mixture between bowls and colour with purple, pink and orange gels.
f) To layer, gently spoon first layer into serving glasses. Chill for 5-10 minutes. Repeat with the rest of the layers.
g) Refrigerate until needed. When serving, allow to stay in room temperature for 15 minutes.

DRINKS

92. Toasted S'more Martini

Makes: 4 servings

INGREDIENTS:
- 1-ounce dark chocolate or milk chocolate liqueur
- ½ ounces fluffed marshmallow vodka
- ½ ounce heavy cream
- Hershey's chocolate syrup and crushed graham cracker for the rim
- marshmallows as garnish
- small bamboo sticks

INSTRUCTIONS:
a) Dip the rim of your glass in the Hershey syrup and then in the crushed graham cracker.
b) Pour the chocolate liqueur as slowly as possible over an upside-down spoon into the glass.
c) Mix the heavy cream and marshmallow vodka in a separate container.
d) Pour the vodka mixture as slowly as possible over an upside-down spoon to make the layered look.
e) Place the marshmallow on the bamboo stick as a skewer.
f) Brown the marshmallow slightly over an open flame.
g) Lay the bamboo stick on the drink and light the marshmallow for effect before drinking. stir together the drink and enjoy!

93. Baileys S'mores

Makes: 2 servings

INGREDIENTS:
- 100ml Baileys Original Irish Cream
- 100g crumbled digestives or shortbread
- 100g mini marshmallows
- 120g marshmallows
- 100ml chocolate sauce
- Blow torch to finish

INSTRUCTIONS:
a) Add the crumbled shortbread to the bottom of a jar. Dollop on marshmallows.
b) Heat the chocolate sauce and pour it into the jars. Probably add a bit more chocolate sauce.
c) Sprinkle on the mini marshmallows.
d) Pour the Baileys over your creation.
e) Now toast the marshmallows with the blow torch until melty and delicious.

94. Ghost Busted Cocktail

Makes: 4 servings

INGREDIENTS:
- Sugar, Rimming
- Marshmallow, Eyeballs
- ¼ cup sugar
- ¼ teaspoon Pure Vanilla Extract
- 10 drops of food color
- 1 large marshmallow
- 2 drops of food color
- ½ cup heavy cream
- 2 tablespoons simple syrup
- 1-ounce vodka
- 1 teaspoon Pure Vanilla Extract
- ¼ cup club soda

INSTRUCTIONS:
a) For the Rimming Sugar, mix sugar and vanilla on a small plate. Add food color; mix until sugar is evenly tinted. Wet rim of beverage glass with water. Dip the rim of the glass into black sugar to lightly coat.

b) For the Marshmallow Eyeballs, cut marshmallows crosswise in half. Place 1 drop of food color in the center of the cut-side of each marshmallow half.

c) Fill the cocktail shaker two-thirds full with ice. Add cream, simple syrup, vodka, and vanilla; shake until well mixed and chilled. Strain into rimmed beverage glass. Top with club soda. Garnish with Marshmallow Eyeballs. Serve immediately.

95. <u>Marshmallow Popcorn Milkshake</u>

Makes: 2 servings

INGREDIENTS:
- 1 cup whole milk
- ⅔ cup popcorn
- ½ cup mini marshmallows
- ⅔ cup vanilla ice cream
- ¼ teaspoon salt

INSTRUCTIONS:
a) Place the popcorn in a blender and pulse until the popcorn becomes like a fine breadcrumb.
b) Then add the marshmallows, milk, and ice cream. Blend until smooth.
c) Taste the milkshake and see how tastes first without the added salt.
d) Then add the marshmallows, milk, and ice cream. Blend until smooth.
e) Taste the milkshake and see how tastes first without the added salt.

96. Blackberry Marshmallow Cream Soda

Makes: 4 servings

INGREDIENTS:
- 1 shot of Blackberry Simple Syrup
- 1 shot of Gin
- Soda Water
- 1 big dollop of Marshmallow Fluff

MARSHMALLOW FLUFF
- 1 10 ounces bag of Dandies Mini Marshmallows
- Liquid from 1 can of Chickpeas
- 1 teaspoon Coconut Oil

INSTRUCTIONS:
a) Fill a glass with ice. Pour in 1 shot of blackberry simple syrup and a shot of gin, and stir. Fill the rest of the way with soda and top with a dollop of marshmallow fluff.

MARSHMALLOW FLUFF
a) In a stand mixer whip aquafaba until fluffy peaks form in the meringue. Meanwhile, in a microwave-safe bowl combine coconut oil and marshmallows. In 30-second intervals, giving a quick stir between each, microwave until the marshmallows have fully melted.
b) Add the marshmallow mixture into the stand mixer with the meringue and whip together until smooth.
c) Store in an air-tight container in the fridge for up to 5 days.

97. Ginger Peaches and Cream cocktail

Makes: 4 servings

INGREDIENTS:
- 1 ounce Bourbon
- ½ ounces Peach Schnapps
- Ginger beer
- Bourbon-Brûléed Dandies Marshmallow, for Garnish

INSTRUCTIONS:
a) Fill a glass with ice. Add 1 shot of bourbon and ½ shot of peach schnapps.
b) Top the rest of the glass with Ginger Beer and stir. Garnish with a Brûléed Dandies Marshmallow.
c) Place a marshmallow on a skewer, dip it in bourbon, and roll in sugar.
d) Using a kitchen torch or flame from a gas stove, toast the marshmallow until the sugar turns into a burnt crust.

98. Lemon Meringue Pie Cocktail

Makes: 4 servings

INGREDIENTS:
- 1-ounce Vodka
- ½ ounces Amaretto Liqueur
- 1 tablespoon Simple Syrup
- 1 ounce Lemon Juice
- 1 dollop of Marshmallow Fluff
- Crushed Graham Cracker

INSTRUCTIONS:
a) Fill a Martini shaker with ice. Add simple syrup, lemon juice, vodka, and Amaretto liqueur.
b) Shake vigorously for one minute.
c) Dip the rim of a martini glass into lemon juice and then into a crushed graham cracker.
d) Pour strained alcohol into the martini glass and top with a dollop of marshmallow fluff.
e) If you have a kitchen torch, torch the fluff for some extra flair.

99. Liquid Smore Cocktail

Makes: 4 servings

INGREDIENTS:
- 1 shot of Marshmallow Vodka
- 1 Tablespoon chocolate syrup or liqueur
- 1 shot Irish Cream
- 2 shots half & half

INSTRUCTIONS:
a) Pour the chocolate syrup into a cocktail shaker.
b) Add the vodka and Irish Cream.
c) Add 1 shot of half and half.
d) Fill the shaker the rest of the way with ice and shake well.
e) Pour into a martini glass dipped in cream and crushed graham crackers.
f) Top with the remaining half and half.

100. Strawberries and marshmallow cocktail

Makes: 4

INGREDIENTS:
- 8 white marshmallows
- 4 raspberries
- 1L strawberry ice cream
- ½ cup cream liqueur, chilled
- ⅓ cup vodka, chilled
- 125g raspberries, extra
- 1 teaspoon vanilla bean paste

INSTRUCTIONS:
a) Preheat the grill to medium. Line a baking tray with foil. Thread the marshmallows and raspberries onto small bamboo skewers. Cover the exposed ends of the skewers with foil. Place on the lined tray.

b) Cook under the grill for 1-2 mins or until the marshmallows are lightly toasted.

c) Place the ice cream, liqueur, vodka, extra raspberries, and vanilla in a blender and blend until smooth and creamy. Pour evenly among serving glasses.

d) Top with the marshmallow skewers and serve immediately.

CONCLUSION

Sticky, sweet, and hard to resist, marshmallow recipes aren't just for kids anymore! There's just something comforting about marshmallows, no matter how they're served! Enjoy these 50 recipes that put a creative twist on your childhood favorites.